THE GEM IN EYE

Poems and Thoughts

Rollo Reese

This is dedicated to my grandma who told me to extend myself. She told me to believe in my ability. I hope this inspires you to believe in yours!

CONTENTS

MOTTO

Remember Where I Came From
Because I Gotta Keep Going I Can't Give in
I Made it Out so I Won't Waste My Opportunity
I Will Sleep When I'm Dead
I Set the Tone on How I Want to Live
And I Will Live How I Feel
I Will Never Be Just Normal
When Everyone Else Stops I Will Keep Going
Because I Know My Limits "I Have None"
All I Ever Wanted Was Peace In My Life
In Order to Do That I Have to go Farther
I Have to go Further
Tell my Story
Leave my Mark

GEM IN EYE

I should no long question the why,

No need to fake it or lie I have it in me to try,
watching on the sidelines I just might cry

I've spent long enough being shy, if I can't do it
now I might as well sit on my bed and die

my frenemies laugh behind my back, to my face they say hi

waiting for my efforts to burn up or fry

judging me... waiting for my dreams that are full
of life, to lose their fluidity and to dry

saying " I told you so", after waiting
around the corner like a spy

Looking at me like I'm a criminal knowing that
I'm alone, no accomplice, no alibi

In the end only I alone will sit in my chamber, the fall guy

but I'm not the only one that feels that life has me on standby

Many reading this right now may feel like
things have passed them by

We are in this together lets continue to support
and encourage, yes I mean you and I

Believe in yourself build brick by brick, if at

first you fail it's okay to sigh

*I promise you it gets better keep going you'll
shine & get your piece of the pie*

everyday is a new chance for change, a retry

*The world's opinions change learn to stay
focused, ignore and defy*

*All that ever matters is to always bet on yourself... self-
visualization, it all starts with you, the Gem in Eye*

IN

There once was a person who hid everything inside
Too scared to take control of his life and decide
The game of life he felt he couldn't win
Stress, and anxiety soon crept in
Was this the life he dreamed... I think he lied

UN-PERFECTION

*Nobody laughs at me long enough Nor do they even
think about me long enough… For me to watch
my life go by for trying to be too nice*

*to everyone because I want them to know
that I have it all together*

*Even if that means I paralyze myself to
ignore all of my goals and*

*leave them in my dreams so that I can drink them away with a
glass of anxiety because I'm too scared to make a mistake*

*So that I pretend to be perfect until it makes me
depressed crazy and resentful because it is the
right thing to do per society for anybody else*

*While I pack all my true feelings up and put it back there
somewhere on the shelf
What is there to live for if I fall in line like everyone else*

I'm gonna do want I must to not care about rejection

*I don't care about your ranking I'm not
interested in your selection*

*I'm talking to myself I don't care about
your acceptance or perception*

I'm just done with this lie of perfection

I feel so much better now. I think I'm going to write a book or a poem or something beautifully unperfected! ..

BACK (THE SAME OLE)

I'm back to the same place with my back against the wall feeling backed up in a corner right back to where I belong.... I'm going backwards to the same place I was yesterday today and tomorrow in circles... in rewind. I'm all alone no one that has my back no support at all with enough stress to cause me back pain as I hunch over. Why is it the same thing, different time, different year but, the same thing. I just know I was making progress. Why can't I get back up to fight. I'm deflated no backbone to face the challenge or the fears. I'm consistently at the backend of progression. Can I snap out of this and get back to some type of reality... back to life! As I step back and look beside myself from the background, I remember my backstory. It's always been the same thing just a different challenge for a different day right back to the future... So yeah I've made it this many years I can leave my seat backstage and quarterback this moment. No more backsliding or backpedaling just take a few steps forward, afterwards I can back my way out of this. So Instead of putting myself back in the corner I'm going to take the backstreets I know to show me what I already know. All this other noise is in the background (distractions). All of a sudden I awake. Everything is still the same... guess I will ignore everything I dreamed and go back to sleep.

RUNNING OUT
OF TIME

Running ducking scared too
I'm humming sucking air too
There is nothing fucking fair
Because becoming something compared to
All this judging discussing dare to, ...become great,
The pressure got me slugging grudging not wanting to share who... I am
I'm just bugging clutching impaired
Now I'm aging so I'm rushing trucking ahead
Time isn't promised so I better get to loving becoming instead
Time is short so I gotta keep drumming budding prepared
I have little time for conducting constructing or to un-bare
Even less for discussing time is shutting and the time I lost I can't repair!
I know this isn't touching, my time is cutting... looks like I erred

THE STRESS
OF IT ALL

10 1/2 Cups of Managing *(Add more at the end to make a harder crunchy exterior)*

2 Drops of Credit extract *(more than 2 drops will over power)*

3 Cups of Sleep *(room temperature)*

2 Table Spoons of Listening *(too much and you will have to start over)*

1 Spoon of Other Peoples Responsibilities *(extract...this is optional your preferred taste)*

1/4 Cup of Social Media (cubed miscellaneous ingredients)

1 Cup of Packed Process Food *(evaporated)*

1 Pack of Motivation *(shredded)*

A Pinch of Dreams (more for garnish)

SOUL HATES

I thought we were suppose to be soul mates
But during our time I heard my soul waits
Foundation was broken by karma so my soul aches
Just so you could play with my heart to try and make my soul break
All so you could test the boundary of what limits a soul takes
I gave you my heart and all you wanted to give me was soul fakes
I guess your soul was already broken so you stabbed me in the heart
multiple times with the pieces of your soul flakes
You craved power and didn't care what damage your soul makes
I slowed things down and in the background my soul could feel the
forsake
My mind and soul talked it out and gave my heart a soul shake
I took your dark energy recycled it to make it clean so that my soul
would wake
I learned to forgive you and forgive myself and watch my character soul
shape
My heart has compassion for you but love from you will never get
through because you are the one my soul hates

SHE THINKS

She thinks she makes him laugh
He thinks he's found the path
She thinks she's the reason they fall
He thinks he's climbing the wall
She thinks she knows what he's up to
He thinks no analyze & would love too
She thinks it's entertaining and cute
He thinks puzzles & games are the route
She thinks but gets distracted by the rain
He thinks in her life she will be always glad he came!
He thinks she loves this message so clear
She thinks " a poem, fuck outta here"

DAD

I just don't know where to start ....

Umm........ I don't have any questions

Where do I start ....(heavy sigh, deep breath)

That's why we come from women cause you aren't even around

I'm not mad I don't even know that you exist

This is for all those dads that disappear leaving their kids to grow up pissed.

While the moms raise them, knowing that the other part of them is being missed

**Not being apart of your kids life is a complete diss
knock some sense into you punch you with a fist
I'm not even mad I don't even know that you exist.**

Man.... I gotta overcompensate for you my whole life

All this time my relations problems were partly because of you with my old wife

You gotta be kidding me

Subconsciously getting rid of you is getting rid of me

You are the 99th problem on my list

All these years it's in my DNA I can't resist

get the fuck away from me with that negativity I insist

**Not being apart of your kids life is a complete diss
Knocks some sense into you punch you with my fist
I'm not even mad at you I don't even know that you exist**

COLD CUTS

It's been *chilly* ever since the start. I've been serving up the same *sandwich* for years. *Lettuce* call it the cold cut combo. Every chance I get instead having the guts to choose some variety, you guessed it, I freeze up and play it safe by choosing *turkey*. No *cheese* for me I just want it *plain*, how predictably boring. For my drink I choose *water* with a lot of ice to drown my sorrows from lack of courage to order what I really want. All these years in front of me I see the *combo* I want. If this story is the *beef* you can tell i'm getting *roasted*. It's *Salami* to fix this! You know what? Let's switch it up. It's my life so I need to be an active participant and *chip* in. I need to *mustard* up the courage to order exactly what I want and be specific. I need to *pepper* up my life. Did I lose you....Don't get all *salty* on me now, not all of us have been *cured*. I'm just being the change I want to see… a *ham!* None of this is any good if I don't try a few *spreads. I* need to sample these first to get the right combination, I want the whole *tomato.* Oh wow, I'm starting to fill a little chilly again. Actually, on second thought, I'll have the *chicken* salad to eat instead, it's just so *plain* good. By golly I like this chicken salad combo no really I do (gulp). I'm gonna get it to go please." I'm gonna put it in the fridge and save it for later. I seem to cherish the misery, I like my life served up *cold*.

ENLIGHTEN ME

Frighten me so good that it Enlightens me
Enlighten me so good that it rightens me
Thundering so good I need lightening
I want a challenge so good that it chess tightens me
Motivate me so good that I can see the fight in me
Something that taste so good that
you can see the bite in me
Making me reach farther than before that it heightens me
Turns me from a soldier and Knightens ME... Titans ME
Curiosity that shines so bright that I
can see the light in me...

BURNING OUT

I'm tired of being done and
　　I'm done with being tired
I have nothing to drive my energy and
　　I have no energy no drive....
Is working for someone this hard all there is,
　　I doubt it ..as it's hardly working
Is the American dream what it use to be or
　　Maybe I need to think bigger by dreaming the American way
I don't want any freebies,
　　But I *want to be free and live*
The burning inside me is to be great and
　　Yet the burning I show outside is stress, fear and comfort..
Is there any light to save my candle or
　　Is this all turning out to be just melted wax?

ADDICT (TO MY WIFE)

"You are my kind of weather

Your scent, the smell it just pulls me in your direction

You give me so much energy and adrenaline it's
hard to come down from these clouds

I just can't get enough I want more and more and
the same amount no longer has any affect

I never thought I would ever do drugs but
then you came into my life and

Instantly like the wind you blew me away

Yeah I'm your addict!"

LEGENDS OF THE FALL (THE FALLEN)

Are you looking for me, why? So you can tell me I told you so. Am I your entertainment? Is it weird to not be able to find me. Did you expect me to be somewhere crying. Thinking my last failure would have me dying. I have to be somewhere lying on the ground right. Oh those failures were just to create the foundation. So how come you didn't see me on the hill over there at my destination. Look up, not down.. I was over there at the cliff... you just missed me. I was just sitting there and an opportunity just fell right into my lap. I was right there, I took a leap into the water right where the legends....

JEALOUS ONES

Roses are red violets are blue
Be careful of what you think you are gonna do!
Don't be so fast to brag because **I RAISED YOU!**

All of these things you have because **I PAID YOU!**
All of the game you have **I GAVE YOU!**
All of this life you have because **I SAVED YOU!**
Your squeaky clean image you have
because **I BATHED YOU!**
The road that you are taking **I PAVED FOR YOU!**
All of the attention you have because **I PARADED YOU!**
Who was your biggest fan first **I RAVED YOU!**
And all these people continue to **PRAISE YOU!**
I provided all of that and what **YOUR**
HEART CRAVED TOO!
Remember all that you have is **BECAUSE I MADE YOU!"**

SPACE

I need _____ , you know!! For me to_____ you know!!
Maybe i want to _____ . I might even_____. I kinda of
thought I would_____ . So that i can be _____. Then
I'm going to _____ This is all really_____ for me...
I spaced out, I don't remember the whole point of this
conversation.

PIECES

I don't want to be involved. I don't want no piece of your drama. I have enough drama on my own. I don't want to answer for you I don't want to pick up your slack. You made your bed now you lay in that story that scene that video. I created this bubble I worked on it hard for years I worked to earn the right for my privacy my space. I took what you made me handle. Now my body and soul need a rest. **You are disturbing my peace.**

I felt like I lived a whole lifetime in 3 to 5 years. I'm an old soul I had to grow up young. In that time I saw pain and I saw suffering. I experienced pain and suffering and I dished out my pain so that others could feel my suffering. I didn't know if I would every find a way out. I just wanted what was normal. I just wanted to play I wanted to dream. I didn't want to worry about finding food, water and lights. I just wanted to enjoy my time. I wanted to be a kid. I wanted to be human like everyone else, no noise and no drama Everywhere we moved it seemed like the same ole drama. At first I blamed myself but there was one final move that told me I could be better. That there was better, that I could learn and grow and be accepted. Like there was a **piece** of the pie of life out there for me. **Finally I could rest because I was at peace**.

Some things are worth fighting for. The life i choose to live is one of them. I say all I want is **peace** in my life. **Peace** doesn't mean to sit still. **Peace** doesn't mean being lazy. **Peace** is to find my path and when I find my way to keep **growing** keep shining and keep **glowing.** Then I take what I learned no hiding and no **slowing.** I will enlighten others to be the example and I'll be the example with my actions by **showing. I'll** show them how to put their own puzzle together just by giving them a **few pieces** of my puzzle like my elders have done before me. As I get older I learned that even with the help from others it is up to me to make and **find my own peace to no end, so I will keep going....**

REAL OR FAKE

Tell me is it real or is it fake... let's figure it our with my mind before I end up with heartache

Your intentions did you fail to mention what type of heart incisions you want to make. Are you really that into me or do you want to just take my energy, until you are my enemy a lots at stake. Help me lose all my friends wondering what got in to me. After all you ain't no kin to me. Are you trying to introduce sin to me? Your smile says lets do this together. You laugh like I'm the best joke forever. Your eyes say we can handle any kind of weather. I'm eyeing your actions to see whether I can handle this forecast. So..

Tell me is it real or is it fake... let's figure it out with my mind before I end up with heartache.

Is this really what people think, is everything that is everything a reality or did I just miss the wink? Is everything fair and on level playing field or am I on the boat you all castaway? I'm cancelled so now I'm suppose to be quiet to sink and not see another day. Do I have a seat or not? If I'm late to the reality can you save me a spot? Are we so cruel that kindness is forgot? Does there always have to be a fight with the have and have nots If I'm not the one on top? Or is it the ones that are afraid they are no longer the cream of the crop? Are they too selfish to see their own stock drop or do they continue to use others like a stand-in or a prop? If I'm at the bottom am I jealous or envious of all this slop? Over here playing good cop bad cop, eating my own shit like it's the best of all that drops. Are we afraid to take accountability at the next stop? Rather make excuses all the time instead of filling my garden with carrots I can pick up at the next hop. Instead I don't want to grow carrots, I want someone to take me to the fancy carrot shop. Where they were smart enough to take someone else's carrots make them shine so much that they can markup the price for every shine that pops. Only to discuss if it matters to everyone what's really real about these carrots and what's really not.... Is this reality!

Tell me is it real or is it fake... let's figure it out with my mind before I end up with heartache

REST

Reset   **R**eposition   **R**elax   **R**echarge

Ease up   **E**xtract   **E**xhale   **E**xit

Slowdown   **S**immer down   **S**leep   **S**top

Turn around   **T**urn down   **T**une out **T**urn off   **Now!**

I HAVE NO CHOICE

(but to follow my dreams)

Pros (8)

Live the unique life I choose to live -
Challenge myself to be great - don't wait
Figure out how to win in life (take chances)
Speak up for my truth- don't be weak
Create My Own Path (my world)
Inner peace and balance
Follow my dreams into reality
I succeed (freedom)

Cons (.......∞.....)

All my fears are attacking me - stress, anger & anxiety
All my dreams and visions start to haunt me - can't ignore them entirely
People laughing at me - people will always laugh I see
Brain and heart neglect me - for wasting my talent disrespectfully
My veins are clogged with the stress - years of ignoring my dreams I'm a mess
High blood pressure - killing myself softly
I will fail
Hide behind social media, tv and video games
Be quiet and listen to what I'm told to do
Work on other's dreams
Become disgruntle
take my dreams to the grave
Be jealous of others
Envy what others have
Become depressed
Start to worry all the time
Hate everyone
Hate everything
Regret not doing it earlier
Running out of time
getting too old
overthinking things
become unmotivated
live the same life as everyone else.
have no voice
have no choice
I'm crying y'all
help me change my mind
oh what could have been
I wish I would have done something
now I'm stuck here......

THE GYM AND I

Damn Life is a Bench
So why are you pressing me to get it together
I'm inclined to get to the club, just give me a couple of minutes to get out of bed
I hate being roped into things I need a little freedom I'll get there in a minute
I'm just gonna curl up for 15 minutes more until the snooze alarm goes off
Lets see how long I can stretch this time out until I have to get up
This is my routine that I cycle through... one of these days it will work
I just need to warm up before I get out of bed since it's cold outside
Weight a minute I'm almost ready.
I just need a few more reps of sleeping/snoozing
You don't need to put me at the end of the plank I'll be up shortly
On second thought I decline the personal invitation to the club I'm going back to sleep
Where are the cables I mean wires to this alarm clock
I'm clamping down on this decision
One of these days I will be pumped to get started
I know I need to form these habits for health sake
Just save me a spot please
I think my will power has resistance
This isn't cutting it I need to make a change

.

OUT

Let Me Just Speak Out loud
So Get Out of My Face
I'm Taking a Time Out
I'm Going Out There to See for Myself
Time to Test the Outer Limits
Of my Outer Space
Nothing is Out of Bounds
My Happiness Outweighs Everything
All This Other Shit is Garbage Anyway
So Let me Take it Outside
LET ME OUTTA HERE!
….My Heart is Fired Up I'm Becoming Outrageous

COLORS

Yellow! How are you?

Orange you glad I came ?

The day blue by!

Don't you a green?

You red my mind!

CAISSIER (THE CASHIER)

I always see you, but at the time it did not register

of recent every time we talked I was more interested as to
who you are, I believe I'm buying into what you are selling

I believe in moments and I felt not embracing
the moment I would surely pay for it

Knowing that time is money I wrote you
a note so that I could get change

Does that make sense.

LEGENDS OF THE FALL... (IN LOVE)

Orange you glad to see me....
I met you for a reason, I guess it was the right season.
Lets stay calm let me ease in.
How do I talk to you a message here or
two I will start feeding..
nothing crazy just a little teasing
I know it was our first meeting..
in an effort to meet up, of course when
that chance comes I'm treating,
I'm cutting the line to get to the front
bobbing and weaving.
But I have to show you in me that you can believe in
It's September I guess you can say I've *"Fall-in" in love and I'm not leaving.*

HEARTLANDS

I promise I will take great care of your heart
I will always treat it like a work of art
So that it always smiles when it's with me
In such a way that it will never forget me

I now know that it's never too late
My heart feels it's found a true soul mate

It won't matter if you ever ignore me
Because in your heart you will always
know the truth to this story

BOX

Don't put me in a corner. Don't put me in your circle. Don't fold me into your labels. Don't try to glue me together. I don't want to be closed up. Can't you just appreciate me for who I am. Don't assume you already know the answer to my riddle cuz you don't really know what's inside. Can't you listen to what I say. Just be in the moment for once. If you can't do that, we might as well square up. My line is too long for you to cut me off. Sit down, listen and learn it's my time to shine and I have a lot to unwrap.

BECAUSE I GOTTA KEEP GOING I CAN'T GIVE IN

When I was younger it felt like nobody cared
Why did everyone else seem really
happy and how is that fair
As I held in those tears and closed off my heart to repairs
You were laughing at me I was a kid
why did you all have to stare
The misery we were dealt why is it my pain alone to bear
When I was younger that would be me
slumped over in a chair
but as I got older I took deep breaths
and began to clear the air

The air that I released allowed the healing to begin
I noticed that we are all unique, to be
comfortable in my own skin
I had to believe that none of that was the end
I had to believe no matter what that I could win
I had to believe that even if my chances
of success were slim
I had to believe I could change my focus and transcend
Because I gotta Keep going I can't give in

(No Matter What!)

32

THE THREE OF US

**It was just the 3 of us ....You, me and us.........
And we are the 3 I trust**

This is the story of us that I **remember**.....
days were slow, long and cold like it was always **December**...

We had very little water and **food** yet we had gratitude,
and we never whined and were never **rude**

Our neighbors would let us use their water **hose**.....
for thirst and so that we could hand wash our **clothes**

Yet those early days as kids we were fine **together**
We were 3 of a kind **together**

**It was just the 3 of us ....You, me and US.........
And we are the 3 I trust**

I was the shy one, my brother was the funny sly
one and my sister was the "I **know**"

I really started to change, my raw emotions began to **show,**
Unnecessary issues affected our family, way more than the **status quo**

I couldn't stand by and watch our future be compromised,
NO! To save us 3 I had to take a stand and so we had to **go**

We were only kids we deserved better, no hurt again
ever, that is why my top had to **blow**

and then

**It was just the 3 of us ....You, me and us.........
And we are the 3 I trust**

Dealing with the aftermath we were going down separate paths our emotions were at all time **highs.**

The pain and constant neglect became everyones fury to correct, we needed love for our heart **cries**

I promised myself I would get it together and no one could hurt us again for whatever so i would **keep a look out with both eyes**

We weathered the storm together our bond is stronger than ever we are now able to handle any endeavor the struggle has made us **wise.**

and it will always be just the 3 of us ....you, me and us.........and we are the 3 I trust

VULTURES

I should be ashamed of myself for not seeing it all sooner. Who plucked your feathers. We all have needs and use each other a little, but damn do you want to take all of me. Do you want to take all my resources, all my time, all my creativity and all my life so that you can live sort of happy. Even that's still not enough for ya. You don't even have power, you are so weak that you can't be alone with yourself. You want me to be on your level so you want to suck all of my blood out too. Why do you want to take my breath away. Why do you want to knock me out of the sky while I'm flying high. Why don't you have it out with all of the other vultures and you guys can scavenge over each other. It is sickening how you twist and manipulate things. Why can't you be honest with me or yourself. Don't be fake, just say what you want. Why waste your life when you can help me waste mine right? Oh wait,.... **You think I'm already dead.**

NEW YORK

SkyScraping,
heart-aching,
Pizza Makin,
Culture Appreciation,
International Representation,
Music Creation,
Talking Perfectly Illustrating,
Talk, Tell it How it is Straightening,
Storytelling and Authentic story creation,
Visionaries and Ideation,
Music Swag Personification,
Stay Awaken,
Best Sport Fan Celebrations
Festival Blazen
Always Outside, No Stay In
Subway Taking
Hotdog Inhalation
Food Selections you Craving
Wine, Dine and Best Steak-in
Bold Blunt Respect Demanded and is Never Forsaken
Historically Relevant and Spoken to with Articulation
Instant Amazement and Gratification
Best City by My Calculation
NEW YORK CITY... Anything else "fuhgettaboutit"

ME

With all that is in me
I promise to defend me
to utilize what's within me
To respect and commend me
To the moon I will send thee
to always make myself the prize to win me
to never let someone else's opinions
take power over or offend me
to always praise and recommend me
To persevere and transcend me
to not waste all that you give me
To always and forever live me
until I use all that is in me
and the lord decides to end me

MISUNDERSTOOD

I'm not like you, or am I? I'm the same color on the outside, but am I the same color on the inside. Does my voice say we are different? Does my height? Maybe it's where I'm from. Do I have to live in the ghetto to be able to find my rhythm? Do I have be rich to have any intellect? Who cares what continent I was born in, are you listening because it seems you already made your mind up. They say believe a person the first time when they tell you , but you didn't even give me that chance. I'm not selling what you think you are buying from me. What if I like that club or that gang or that music or that video game. I'm just an artist like anyone else trying to draw your attention to what I'm saying. Every art is different, yet some of the same themes remain. If you take time to see the art for what it is then you get it. Yet you are quick to throw me away based on what someone else says. When you haven't even heard or listened to me talk. I didn't say I need anything from you but your attention, I didn't ask for money or time. I'm not gonna hurt you. I'm not trying to buy you, i'm not trying to hit on you. Can you just listen with your ears and I need you to listen with your eyes too. Please fix your body as I don't understand what language it's speaking to me right now it's all gibberish. Maybe I would't be here if you wouldn't have pointed me out in the first place. Maybe instead of ignoring me you could have tried to understand you've seen me enough times to know something is up or wrong. Or just maybe it's me personally assuming what everyone thinks or not, maybe I need to put myself in check. Maybe I need to ask anyone else if they understand me or tell them I need help. How can they understand from my body language? Maybe I need to just talk and close my eyes from listening and just take one step towards the middle. Because maybe...just maybe.... I misunderstood you too!

LIKE

Like New Is to York

Like fries are to hamburgers

Like Water is to a desert

Like Sugar is to "Hey Honey"

Like Turkey is to Ham

Like Bruce is to Lee

Like Sun is to glasses

Like swim is to ing

Like Grilled is to Cheese

Like U is to R

Like Arm is to Me or the Navy

Like Tears are to Fears

Like Barbie and Ken

Like Mustard is to Ketchup

Like Husband is to Wife

Like May is to Be

Like Social is to Media

Like you and Me

WE are all "a" like for someone or somehow did that "click" (Already Verified)

PEACES

In the name of peace I can shield myself from everyone's projections
In the name of peace I can't shield me from myself there is no protection
In the name of peace myself is the only cure and I'm the diseased weapon
In the name of peace I have to go after what my heart feels destined.
In the name of peace I'm gonna try to solve this life equation
In the name of peace I will let go and find ways to let the suns rays in
All I've ever wanted is peace I say this with endless desperation

MACRO MANAGER

Manager your way in
Manager your way out
Manage them out
Did you Manage to engage them
Your Management style doesn't fit the culture
It's the managers fault
Employees always leave the Manager
I don't know? you are the Manager
How did you Manage to do that
Lets bring that up to Senior Management
I'm going to promote you to Manager
I'm the Manager here
These are Managerial duties
You are my favorite Manager
You are the worst Manager
I hate Micro Managers
Managers don't get paid OT
That's why you make the big bucks
Oh no!!!.... that's the Managers job
I can't work OT today
Hello final warning
Lets be positive today
Let's boost moral
I have some team building for ya
Not sure i wanted to be Manager in the first place
How did I Manage to get here
Why does it feel like I'm all alone
Managers list always expands
It's the Managers fault
I expect you to fix it
Time Management is key for all the projects i'm giving you
Can you take on this as well
This function fits better with you
Hey there new Manager, lets give you these employees as well
Can i ask you a question, how did you Manage to figure this all out

I TO EYE

EYE feel like I've seen way too much.. So I close my eyes so they can ignore what's cold in this world and so my eyelids can warm them. While I'm warming them up, everything is slow-motion. I start to see all these colors on my eyelids in the dark like I'm in another galaxy and right when it goes completely dark I occasionally dream, but it is always of what I've seen that same day. So then it turns to anxiety and my eyes can't shut it off . Then I open them back up because they are addicted to distractions. I try to ignore what I have seen in my dreams. I also try to ignore what my eyes are suppose to do like concentrating on my goals as my eyes are eager to work. So since I'm not doing that and they are eyeing a computer screen seeing all the screen shots of garbage my eyes start to dry out. I also, get a headache so then I have to close them so they can get warmed up again but this time I listen to what they want to see. I go outside I take a walk, I look at the sky, I look at the trees, and I see the sounds they are looking for... a reset. That's when instead of two eyes, my insight kicks in and I see what I'm suppose to do.

MOM - MOM (GRANDMA)

It still HURTS like hell, but I will be okay. That's what I would tell her if she could hear me. It hasn't been a month since you've passed yet, but your presence or just your spirit is so missed.. Look at how strong you made me!!! I miss your words, your guidance and your support. I MISS YOU!! says my tears..... I've tried to hide my feelings act like things are normal but they aren't yet ....I'VE NEVER FELT ANY SUPPORT LIKE YOURS .....   We were 3 kids by ourselves a long time and you took us in.   I was so lost .. such a lost soul ....so broken so hurt so angry.. I was just a little kid, who could blame me for the way I acted knowing everything I had experienced.....We felt like we had no one to feel our pain and thought no one cared, that's why I acted the way I did for a few years.. we went from place to place until we got to you. You turned this 14 year old filled with anger to one filled with love. I didn't think I would ever get this far. You showed me how to navigate this world and not to make excuses. Right now, I feel alone and I'm so lost again...but this time I know how to find my way. Like you showed me (smile).... I'm almost there...just need a little more time to heal...Love you all the way to the sky. I'm on my way to live the life I choose to live. No excuses like you taught me! Love you Mom-Mom! If anyone ever deserves a shout out from me ....it's you!

GO

Wake up, get up, MOVE, breathe, walk, run, jog, taste, smell live,, try, explore, talk, dance, sing, Do.........Open your eyes

Visualize, see, FOCUS, take notes, plan, draw, map, take action, execute, show, present, repeat.......... DREAM

Conquer pace yourself KEEP MOVING FORWARD plant ,water, nurture, teach, exhale, lift yourself up, deliver results, choose, matter, exist ....YOU GOT THIS!!!

VOWS

When I talk about the most fascinating the most interesting person I've ever known you can see it in my eyes no need to ever question or guess who

*I knew you were the one when I first met you
You tried to friend zone me right after you farted how could I forget you*

In fact our first lunch you really dressed down, but I'm from the streets I like when my lady looks a hot mess "diamond in a rough" which is rare only like a select few

Weeks later you set down in my house talking non-stop and soon after I got a lot of text too

After all that I knew I had to have you I would try my best to

I promise we will always play games you will always win because I let you

I promise to be your biggest supporter and fan because that's what best friends do

I promise you don't have to go at life alone , I'm along for the party like the best dance crew

I promise to listen when you ask me to listen tuned in like a favorite radio station is set to

My grandma said " I like her" and although she is now laid to rest, to replace her love, I now get you

I love you my soul mate my companion you are the closest thing to my heart on my chest like a tattoo…

REALER OR FAKER

Tell me is it really real or is it really fake... let's figure it out with my mind before I end up with heartache

So what about you sucker, you write this have you looked in the mirror what do you proclaim? You are such a lame. You are just the same. You observe does that make you better than others? What have you got left in your name? Are all your failures made up of blame? Are you just gonna keep talking about what you gonna do, "brotha" is this just a game? How can you make it anywhere you are missing the target, no direction, no focus, where is your aim? Time for action, are you ready to build the frame? See all that power out there it's yours to claim. Add all of your "I would" to the fire for more flame. Is this all hearsay just to hear them talk about you to put your name in lights? Is this seriously about vanity and fame? I really think you are a damn shame? It's put up or shut up, how much is this all talk...

Tell me are you really real or really fake lets figure it out with my mind before I end up with heartache

I was little why did you leave, you are all I know. Some say we all have our own demons you were really young you needed to grow. For years I had tears for you they were real in secret I would let them flow. I thought it was all a dream for years and years I hoped you would show. That river flows of tears has dried up because my river bed is too low. I've hardened by my ships gift and curses, mine alone to tow. It's fair to say the ship of hope sailed long time ago. The winds of forgiveness keep my ship floating, everything back here for show. I'm not here to cause you heartache I can tell the demons of my heart fill you with regret. I still have love for you, they say time heals all wounds so to you and I, it's time to let. Can we try another boat, a relation ship, I'm ready to put my feet in the water for a dip. You say you love me I've called you don't call me just to talk I feel like its all service of the lip. Remember you don't owe me anything I take that burden off your hip. Now it's only if you want to open the bag take a chip. I've tried several times and I have forgiven of course but I won't forget. Our roles should be reversed you gotta want this so I hand it over to you mom take the lead switch places flip.

Now tell me are you really real or really fake lets figure it out with my mind before I end up with heartache

REMEMBER WHERE
I CAME FROM

Remember
Childlike, Adventurous
Playing, Dancing Laughing
Always Outside, Friends, No Water, No Lights
Crying, Fighting, Worrying
Broken, Angry
Forget

CRYPTONOMICS

Is it crypto or is it cryptic...
is it like the lotto or more mystic
Either way I missed it
Lost my money real quick

You said this was a new opportunity to go against society's grain
invest in crypto and NFTs get rich without giving my name
honest decentralization all coded on the blockchain
You hacked all my wallets and all this research gave me back pain
Stole a year of my time all to get hooked on you selling me that game

Is this the so called web 3
or did you just spider web me

I reminisce here in your hoodie while I lay here on your rug
All strung out hooked on my new favorite type of drug...

pockets on empty I guess we broke up I'm right where you left me
Theoretically rich on fractional penny tokens and an illiquid NFT

I feel like your crash test dummy
That's what I get for trading time for money

My savings yes I spent it
I'm sticking around until I get it back is my intent
I know what I said so I mint it!

I did mint it. It's for sell.. maybe I will get back my money and then some.....

2ND CHANCES

Preview
Interview
Review
~~Redo~~
We through!

(naw no more chances)

THE "FAIR" WE TELL

You-Them
Please sit down for this quick questionnaire
I mean what's fair is it to be a pair
Only to feel like someone doesn't do their share
I'm just trying to be aware I'm not trying to scare
I feel like your version of equal always leaves
me with a dumb blank stare
am I overthinking this or do you even care
Why on the side of my face do I feel this glare
Like I should be ashamed of what I'm asking, don't you dare
I'm tired of holding it in being the better person I have to clear the air
The stress of it all is that the reason why I have no hair
We need to figure this out before I become a millionaire

Them-You
I understand fair doesn't always mean equal.....
But is it wrong to be fair by making revenge the sequel
you are so damn evil this social contract is deceitful
I'm an eagle why are you treating me like a seagull
I love this torture, fair is meeting me halfway
in a ceremony at the cathedral
That will surely push us to the middle of the fair needle

SOUL MATES

You know that I know, and I know that
you know that I know you feel the same too! My eyes
say I love you. My smile says I want you. My laugh says I need you. You
can feel the heat and the coolness at the same time. Like our closeness
knows and one small touch is so sweet and so gentle it's like our spirits
are magnetically connecting us. It feels so right doesn't it. I just finished
your sentence and you just finished mine. Why does it feel like there
is so much yet so little time for us to feel this moment. Today seems
so endless I'm excited to start tomorrow already. How can this feel so
new yet so familiar at the same time. I'm already drunk on you and I'm
gonna have some more before I have to sober up. That look says it all,
this must be what twins feel like all the time saying the same things
thinking the same things. What a life it must be. I don't want to say
too much because I don't want to ruin the moments here. Cool to watch
it all happen so effortlessly and so naturally. I started to think you
didn't exist. I started to give up hope but when I stopped dwelling on
it my subconscious seemed to have made my wish come true. Are they
playing our song, even the songs I hate right now sounds so fucking
good and so right as we sit here. Love is what this has to be otherwise
i'm just your fool. You are what I wished for. Instead of dwelling I
just listened for a change as you checked off everything on my list.
Our days have been nothing but peace for me, but then again you are a
piece of me. Aren't you a reflection of what I wanted deep down in my
soul. So when it's in the soul it creates more harmony, more realism,
more truism. Not just physical and first impressions, it's pass my soul
teaching me a lesson and it's now showing me what's true and what's
destined.

SHADED

Are we really at this place again.
Do people really hate each other still for their own skin
Are we still killing our souls for democrat, religion or republican
In school people didn't hate you for what club you were in
did anyone use the club to retaliate at your next to kin
Nowadays its so dark instead of understanding
we are just hating or canceling
"You buddy! it's over for one thing wrong your time has to end"
When the definition of a bond use to be a friend that taught lessons
It's seem's we like to hear ourselves talk no resting
Only listening to what other people say just to
use it against them like a weapon

Doesn't matter which side or name we all are to blame
The pattern (there is one) starting to be predictably the same ....
Sometimes everyone being so uniform is boring
The point i'm making is everything is so black,

white or grey we stopped coloring

We need to take a step back and do what artist
do and paint a picture differently
Let colors tell their story and listing and
enjoy the beauty.....endlessly.

(team purple ask me why)

52

I WILL SLEEP
WHEN I'M DEAD

I've Never Slept Well My Mind is Always Racing. Thinking, What Can I Accomplish For The Day For My Life. Trust Me I Can't Shut My Mind Off I Just Keep Going. What's Next, What Else Needs to be Done. Why Didn't I do That. This is a Gift and a Curse I Accept it. This is The Life I Choose to Live. I have No Choice. These are the Principles of My Legacy. Enlighten by Example I'm Living The Unique Life I Choose to Live. Until that is accomplished how can I rest.

CROSS-EXAMINATION

What is your intent

What you say and what you do are different

*You looked me up, down and judged me, it's
starting to feel reminiscent*

*I'm no longer naïve, you have taken my optimism, and
made me guilty even though I'm innocent*

Are your qualifications sufficient

I respectfully dissent

*I thought this was the right opportunity
for me I now know it isn't*

This must be a misprint!

YOU

Don't look at me it's you. Why hasn't anybody done it, because it's for you to do. Why isn't anyone helping, it's for you to help yourself.... Why are you suffering, it's for you to find the cure. It's always been up to you. Why is it such a heavy load. It's for you because you can handle it. You were chosen to do something no one has done, because only your eyes see it and it's stuck in your head. No matter how much you sleep how much you dread. When you wake up or go to bed. You were chosen to fulfill this task. It's the only thing your brain and your heart ask. So take off the mask lose the facade lets make this future better than the past. Now can you choose what's next!

I MADE IT OUT SO I WON'T WASTE MY OPPORTUNITY

I use to stress about what the day was gonna do to me

I remember the days going in circles that sucked usually

I started off as 1 of 3 kids sticking together we had unity

but that wasn't enough for the struggles in life yielded no immunity

I didn't think anyone cared it was just ambiguity

Do you know how it feels to think you were dealt a
bad hand in this world uh such cruelty

.

To feel like it is constantly raining gloomily

and enough worries in the world to make me
want to write my own eulogy

This can't be real it must be an illusory

Like grandmas do they help save the world, she
gave me a sense of community

She showed me how to stop the lunacy

I started to live life with purpose and continuity

I reflect on my past, helping me handle future issues with immunity

Now I build a new life without boundaries… ingenuity

I made it out so I won't waste my opportunity

And I will continue to enlighten others by example in perpetuity

LEGENDS OF THE
FALL (THE LEGEND)

Orange you glad it's not hot anymore...

While we chill, let me tell you about some seasonal folklore

There's this story a select few people tell from as far back as I can remember

They know that some of the most beautiful treasures in the world show off starting in September

As it gets closer their curiosity starts to bolster they gotta get outside of these closing walls

They prepare all year for this, waiting for summer to come to a crawl

Out of this world, if you listen quietly you can hear the calmness call

All slows down and is less crowded in most towns you can see everything no need to be so tall

Not too hot nor too cold it's the most perfect time of the year to embrace the temperature

The leaves change to yellow, orange and red, beauty all around is the signature

The yellow leaves pop out like "hello" to everyone that is currently there

Orange leaves, the color of sunrise and sunset slow things down to a glance and a stare

Couples appreciate mother nature's red leaves symbolizing the love in the air

This season has a variety of lovely things to stumble upon, stare at, or simply have a ball

It's my favorite reason to bring up my favorite season the fairest of them all

The people that believe this and the gift they receive is *"The Legends of The Fall"*

FEARS, PEERS
AND YEARS

I wanted to lose all my fears
I knew I couldn't do that just being in a normal career
That's fine for some, but my heart is the one crying tears

Of sweat and regret, wondering why I haven't gotten started yet
and letting others define my career in their
system is most certainly roulette
In life I only have time for one final proven
strategy, to invest or to bet....

On me, with what I see 5 years of focus into one
thing brings out the best in me
After all anyone in college can do it in 4 to 5
years and they call that a degree
My grandma lived in a tough time and had 5 kids she handled
it fine I'm intrigued... that really messes with me

Through all her struggles she showed us how
to be the best that you can be
She did that with all heart and a smile she wasn't testing me
She didn't tell me what to do as she knows the rest is up to me

Before she left she provided the map, the formula, the blue print
When i talked she smiled, i think i'm on the right path and she knew it.

Now I plan things out for 7 to 10 years and if something feels
off I stop what I'm doing and change the plans screw this!

To everyone out there listen to your family, they say "we
believe you" " be the best you can be" "don't be afraid",
it's you who needs to believe that you can do
it!

LIVING THE DREAM

I don't know about you but I'm gonna go wherever my imagination takes me
Wherever my imaginations makes me
I'm okay if it breaks me
and I will definitely follow it until the end when life erases me

If I dream it grandma says I can most certainly achieve it
Wherever I receive it (blessings)
I'm okay to believe it
and I will definitely take notes and retrieve it

For my dreams I will make the ultimate sacrifice
Wherever I find this vice
I'm okay to roll the dice
and it's definitely worth the asking price

Because life is what dreams are made of naturally
Wherever I find peace proudly
I know I'm okay actually
Because I will live my dream into reality

DIFFERENT

Have you ever felt like you don't fit in but don't fit uniquely out either. That's not quite my scene, but it sort of kind of is sometimes. I agree with you but, I don't agree with that. Like I just want be free of all the stereotypes.. young vs old black versus white, cool vs nerdy or goofy. Can I be a little bit of all of those. Better yet can I be none of those... Maybe I don't want to be labeled, can I just be? Do I have to always pick a side. I don't really like too much of either. I like sitting right here in the middle. It's peaceful right here. This is cool right now but maybe not later. Maybe I love being around you, you and you. Maybe I just want my own space to see my own face. I love my style. I don't care about your point of view don't kill my vibe... Think of me as soda that's already been shaken up too much. I'm just flat without all of the carbonation.

GIRLS OF THE WORLD

How do you do so many things at one time? I can say each and every one of you are interesting to say the least. Adam and Eve, Mars and Venus I believe all stories about you. See I can eat the same thing every day. I can stay in routine every day. I can be oblivious every day. Yet you bring in variety to every day. No way are you eating the same thing after two days. Maybe I need some color in my house or a change of shirts you see that and you don't hesitate to express that so that I know you see more in me you believe in me. You are so detailed, maybe you are better at my job than I am and you give better advice too. You get the engines running inside. I just have to listen that's all you ask. I just have to play, that's all you ask. I just have to include you in what I do that's all you ask. You have such an interesting take on life, sure you get stressed but you carry the workload better and you know how to keep things positive and how to make one entree into 4 meals. That's a game and a bargaining chip. Thank you for letting me be a part of your journey and thank you for letting me be in the front row of your life because being allowed in your presence is an honor an achievement and a compliment.

PEACE BY PIECE

A piece of my heart
A peace of mind
A piece of my soul
A piece of my time

Make room for peace even when everyone is taking a piece of you.

A piece of love
A piece of joy
A piece of happiness
A peace and harmony

Use these pieces as the foundation in guiding you to peace and virtue

A peace from fear
A piece of strength
A piece of purpose
A piece of faith

These pieces matter, when you believe in finding
your own peace from the start

A piece of me
A piece of you
A peace in my dreams
A peace so true

*Find your peace, follow your dreams and **piece***
things together inside your heart

COUSIN

I can't even count all of them I have well over a dozen

It's hard to keep track of the cities all of you was in

Most of us get along great just laughing jokes no fussing

My closest ones I have the most confidence in trusting

*Where are you headed what has called to
your heart like a summon*

*Keep grinding ahead you have my support with
what keeps your heart buzzing*

*The roads are long and you have my ear
when things start to toughen*

*Keeping going further, keep going farther, the
doors of luck will let you bust in*

*When your done lets talk on holiday time while
smelling the food in the oven*

*OMG, Wait is that you cursing, that's what we be
laughing and lovin this is for all of you my cousins*

MY WAY

My shoes, My money, My dreams, My fantasies,
My reality, My actuality,

My happiness, My sadness, My Toughness, My
badness, My War, My Badges

My Action, My Test, My All, My Best, My
Heart , My Chest. My Hug, My Caress, My
Joy, My Carelessness, My Carefulness

My Words, My Choice, My Voice, My views , My
Family, My Accomplishment, My Consequences, My
Fears, My Love, My Success…. fuck the rest,

LESSONS

You are probably right *(instinct)*
Only Once *(no second chances)*
Do you *(instead of everyone else)*
Help in a way that you can *(not always in the way that they want)*
No your role *(most important thing in life)*
Take your chance *(no regrets)*
Give and let go. *(no expectations)*
Dream into reality *(set goals)*
Listen with your eyes too *(stop talking pay attention)*
Relax things take time *(get some rest)*
When you are done you are done *(no second guesses)*
Live and Tell your story *(doesn't have to be like anyone else)*
Stop being scared to be great *(stop with the comfort)*
What everyone else isn't doing, do that *(be yourself)*

I TO I

I hear you loud and clear. I'm done blaming everyone else. I'm done worrying about everyone else. I'm not being selfish then again, yes I am. For so many years I've given, gave away or shared more than I knew I had to offer. I have no regrets, but I do feel like I neglected the one person that matters the most which is myself. I'm a giver by nature but I can't give to anyone until I make myself happy until I matter. Until I believe in myself until nothing no one else says breaks me until I have rewarded myself with a treat. I never put myself first and that effort belongs to me first because I've given that power far too long to people who don't reciprocate good energy in return. I'm worth a fortune if I just use that energy on myself before I give it to others for the half fortunes and quick fixes that they need which isn't enough. It's like they robbed a bank but didn't think it through and so they never have enough. That is not my problem. I can't believe that I let this go on too long that I gave up control that I wondered what everyone else thought internally or externally. Instead of doing what *I* needed to do. Subconsciously I knew this all along *I* just was too scared to face myself.

RAINY

Raining never seems to stop

Raining until everything in life floods over with every drop

Raining while I continue to drown

Raining on everything I do...I just keeping sinking down

Raining I can't walk in my own shoes

It's always raining I continue to lose

Raining making me too scared to go outside

Raining come through the cracks I cannot hide

Raining stop holding it in let out all your cries

The Raining will stop as soon as you dry your eyes.

I'M NOT YOUR COMEDIAN -

You don't think I'm funny ....
But I make you smile

You didn't think I was your type
But I've been here awhile

Well I think you are full of shit
Yet I still clean up the pile

And I can make you laugh, cry, and adore me
I've put this evidence in a file

And with all my annoyance
You still pick up the phone and dial

Save your clap I'm still going
I know you like my swag and style

You thought the first year our fling
Was just a temporary trial

Yet I've known all along
In the future I will scare you by walking you down an aisle

.....Like an aisle to a store... you know

Now ain't that funny.......

STOP SIGNS

I looked at my list I've checked it more than twice. How many STOP signs on my list do I have to cross for me to finally know things aren't right. Is it the first time that you keep going, is it the second time after I told you that it hurts. Is it the third time, that's straight disrespect to myself. I know I'm not happy because it keeps happening, believe them the first time, two people can't tell the same lie. At work is a title all that I lack. Am I working for the love or the money. None of it taste like honey. Do I keep going and going until I reach my breaking point and I lash out and they call me the disgruntle one. Long enough for me to become the bad guy. Better yet I give so much time and dedication to the job by being nice that I have anxiety or a heart attack. Do I have to go out to party all the time. Is it possible to be an addict to that lifestyle. Can I be at the wrong place, at the wrong time saying the wrong thing, hanging with the wrong friends doing the wrong thing, and seeing someone wrongly die to decide it's time to pause. I think these are all great signs for the cause. I should resign from any of these ways of life. When life abruptly slows down in front of you take heed of the lesson. History has always showed me that when that happens it's my one time to make a correction. For me to STOP take a moment, think and go in a different direction. Pay attention to the stop signs as it may be the only chance for you to see your future reflection.

THE GEMINI

What am I suppose to do ... I don't understand...
Should I make a plan or follow the lead
Should I stay quiet or should I speak up
Should I leave or stay or something in between.
Am I suppose to be rich beyond dreams
Am I suppose to help everyone else
Should i just be bored by myself
Maybe I should go and live it up today
Should I ignore them
Should I answer that text message,
Maybe I should read what they say I should do and do that
Maybe I should listen to them right now,
Maybe I should answer the question for them
I think they need help on that, I should really help them
I think about stuff too much,
I think I've seen this before.... wait a minute....
I can't always do that
I can't always be the answer
I can't always be selfish
I can't always be unselfish
I can't always be too nice
I can't always be too stressed
I don't want to
I don't feel like it.
Actually maybe I do feel like it
Lets go ... DO ALL OF IT
Actually Nevermind.
This is exhausting
DO NONE OF IT... sounds better
OMG
I'm still thinking about this …..

AFRAID TO BE GREAT

Why am I afraid to live. I know inside me I have a whole world I have to give. But I stay silent just thinking one day I will be ready. Thinking one day they will let me. Like someone else is the gate keeper to my life. You would think someone has a gun to my brain, better yet a knife and slowly pressing it into my brain. Who are "they".... I don't even know, maybe it's the people that want me to fail. As I think of it...... do they exist. Just as fast as I make them up in my mind, in real life that's how fast they criticize me and disappear ... only seconds. I can ask them do they remember that I'm here, but nobody is watching me, I'm not that important. So what is there to be scared of...people... too many to keep count. Am I too scared that I might succeed, then what? I will have to live a new life, less tv, less wondering what others think. So what I'm saying is that I would rather be comfortable rather then live the way I want to because I'm scared it's gonna be different. What a problem to have, I'm scared to make more money, less money or have more freedom to live the way I truly want to live because I'm scared to not change. Being quiet hasn't gotten me anywhere. All I have to do is focus and do me instead of worry. So which is it, am I too scared to stay the same or am I too afraid to be great.

SETTING **THE** TONE

I set the tone how I want to Live

To Connect and Relate To People
To Laugh Hard
To Travel The Entire World
To Eat Good, but also Eat What I want
To Share but Only When I'm Ready
To Make Time for Myself

AND

I will Live how I feel

The Life I choose to Live
Do only What I Feel is Right for Me
Doesn't Matter What Anyone Else Thinks
If I Don't Like it I Won't Continue to do it I Will Change Course
I Have No Choice.

I SEE IT

When you know you know, they say. When you see it you see it I'm saying…. I just know I see it all in my dreams, and the more I ignore it the less I get to rest. You know what I'm talking about. That thing you want to do but you talk yourself out of because it's so extraordinary it just might be the most fantastic thing to ever happened to you. But…it will disturb the balance of comfort. I don't sleep well anyway but, whenever I put work towards my visions, my anxiety lowers, I feel a little calmer, and I'm just relaxed. I feel like I've seen this my whole life. I was able to block it out for a while but if I stop seeing, it eventually turns into something else like anger, resentment and depression. So one by one I just take the notes and capture them all and put them on a vision board and I see it. I see it into reality and I am always enlightened of what I find out I can do. Most importantly if I look back I see what I have accomplished…. This is what I see… "me in the back of the car all relaxed dressed up in a big city all calm even though I'm going to go give a big speech to a large group of people I'm relaxed because I see them, and I know they see me. It's bigger than that, they actually see what I am seeing." It's never too late to see things into action. It's waiting for me and it's waiting for you to see it through. I see it… don't you?

SANTORINI

Clear skies
for your eyes

believe you me
you will enjoy the scenery

Staying in why bother
go and swim in the blue water

So pretty so white
oh what a sight

You don't have to try hard
every picture you take is a post card

Bring a companion on your arm
to enjoy the charm

Forget all your qualms
and enjoy the calm

If I had one wish from a Genie
I would ask for the chill and calm of a fall day in Santorini

PLAY THE GAME

Play the game Play the game..
The game is all the same
Some say the rules never change
It's something already arranged
I find that to be strange ..
My mindset says that can be rearranged
All that I want is right in my range
So am I just suppose to sit with the rest of you and look all deranged

I'm suppose to sit silent while other people
dictate my life, that is so lame
You better get up and focus it's only your eyes to blame
Why you letting yourself put dirt all up on your name
You just gotta take your space in this world it's yours to claim
Keep playing until you level up be quiet, focus and use your brain
When you learned enough then level up just like any other game....
When you are ready make sure you Aim

Then Fire

GONE

At first I was empty because it felt like you are
gone even when you are with me

Something that no one would envy, took my heart for
granted you tried to steal the power within me So
for now on I will be amicable but not friendly

I just want you out of my life and quickly
I mean that respectfully and sincerely

I just have no emotions at all, is that eerie ....
My brain isn't focused at all on you clearly

any connection to you at all scares me............. It
must be crazy to see me so calm it's really

time to move on so until we... remember each other
so dimly... I'm ready to move on swiftly

not, happy, angry, or sad, just numb to your
actions... I'm gone, I don't care anymore I don't
want to listen and you won't hear me

FUTURE BETTER THAN MY PAST

My future will be better than my past
That's my motto while I'm alive I'll make it last

tapping into my hidden treasures to raid my stash
In the beginning history says I will most certainly crash

If luck doesn't work I will start over, clear my cache
To faux fortune tellers my outlook is going to clash

I will be careful to not look back and get whiplash
My philosophy to others may be too brash and rash
I could care less for your opinions we all have trash.....

Not worried about the divisions you cast
It's my life and I'm gonna have a blast

I got my own goals I'm trying to surpass
my future.. my life... until I'm ash

EARTHQUAKE

Ever since I was little I moved around a lot, city to city state to state. I was a kid so I had to go along for the ride. I always tell people I love travel and I think it's because I moved around a lot so I'm subliminally trying to find my own home. I did not know the impact it would have on me good or bad. See it's hard for me to stay in one position too long because I feel like I need to keep moving. Even if I stay in a place for a while I have to move around the city for a few years to feel balanced. Is this a gift or a curse or something much worse. How does it feel to not ever feel secure believing the ground is gonna always move, your friends will always go and your loved ones will leave? I feel the floor will be pulled from under me if I don't keep moving. I feel life is going too good for me and something bad is destin around the corner. At least I never feel comfortable. I guess I'm never suppose to sit still. I'm starting to think my time on this earth is solely so that I can shake things up.

PROMISE TO MYSELF

I'm making this promise to myself…
That is to live and to live like no one else

Always do thy math
If things don't add up then make my own path

With all that is in me.
Never lose site of my creativity

Continue letting the world unravel
for me that means to never stop my travels

Don't be ignorant to things people ignore
Always be willing to find out for myself to explore

Never settle nothing is ever the end
Continue down the path making sure I extend

Don't forget about loyal family and friends
Never enable them but okay to lend a helping hand

Never treat people with disrespect.
Open your ears so that you can connect

Don't let communication go from black and white to gray
Remember speak up and make sure you have a say

If you find love that is as unique as a piece of art
Love with all of your heart

Don't let life, people, and things get me stressed
And make sure to find time to rest

Even when things don't lead me to a clue
Repeat to myself "Always be you..Always be you"

In my world that I'm still trying to create
Dare to be great Dare to be great

NO MORE TEARS

Get Up Get Up...   Let's do it together...   Let's change the weather
Starting right now and into Forever...........

Dry Them Dry your eyes...   Look up to the skies time to realize
Forget about the worries... your future is out there in disguise

NO MORE NO MORE...   Let go of the pain wash your tears down the drain
I need you to focus. better days are coming so you need to study and train

Time to feel Time to heal... The heartache....   Nothing left to break...
Stand up straight, love is outside in many forms go explore it's never too late....

REASONS

I have No Choice

The Life I Choose to Live

I can't Sleep

I can't shut my mind off

I want to stay forever enlightened

No More Tears

For My Grandma

Promise To Myself

Running Out of Time

I made it out so I won't waste my opportunity

The Stress of it all

I just need Peace.

I set the tone

I live how I feel

Finding my home

Burning out

For the gem in eye

I can keep going but…. Because I want to is actually good enough

SUN

Nature's reminder for the living diers. Open up the windows and the blinds....... Let's get our heads out of the clouds of darkness and let something new luminate the mind. A new spark of interest for our hearts. Just one step that's a great start. It doesn't always have to rain, it doesn't always have to be dark. Just a few more steps, this time let's meet the sun in the park. I feel rays of energy replenishing me back to existence. Let's walk a little more. There is beauty in everything out here. Photogenic flowers and trees, did you know flowers also bloom in the desert. Sometimes we are blinded by the clouds, we may seem alone and deserted, but if we take one step toward any light we get some sort of radiance. Just a little bit of sun will provide us brillance and that will help us grow. After a few months of this natural tanning we won't recognize what a beautiful tree full of life we have become. For these few months we'll be distracted as we cherish the new glow. Then a year will pass and we will forget about everything else except for these sunny days. Now that we've put ourselves out there we are directly in the suns rays nothing to hide, it's all in the light. We are beginning to peel into something so beautiful, so gorgeous and so hot!

LOVE YOU

It hurts to see what you have to go through
and it's hard to see from someone else's shoes
The message is always easier said from others point of view
"Self I wish you best in life cool
Life is tough but take a chance... dive into the pool
Treat yourself with kindness when others are cruel
Don't be everyone else's fool
Learn to be okay being by yourself too
Remember you have to Love you for you"

MOTHERLY

I want you to know that I love you and that:

Memories
Outside
The
Hurt
Eventually
Remain

For the majority of our time together it was:

Mostly
Openhearted
Moments

No telling what I would do for that soul cooked food.. you were:

Making
Amazing
Meals
All the time

That is what I choose to remember spoken better from a kids perspective "mommy you were motherly!"

STAIN

It's like I'm a stain on the world and I didn't even know it. I feel your energy, I walk down the street and I feel something draining me, yet I still fight to keep moving on. I'm just minding my business as happy as can be, but something keeps eating at me. I didn't ask to be this way I was born like this. I want what you want, peace, love and happiness, yet you won't let me be. I can see it in your stare. Let me be clear, I am not your stain! I want to bring greatness in the world. You see me as a threat to your happiness, yet I see room here for all of us. I want to eat explore and learn. I don't want your life I don't want what's yours.

I can hear it in your voice. Let me be clear, I am not your stain! I want to make my own way. In life it takes help from multiple people to achieve the most far out goals. Why must I walk alone. What's wrong with me having a little support. What are you scared of, what if I'm the one that is scared because I'm not accepted because no one cares. Why are you guilting me for your lack of success when you aren't in the light anymore and you fell into a black whole. In fact I don't even know you. I get it...when you see me come from what is perceived as a black hole and turn my struggle into light, you can't handle that and you think you are better. I can sense it in your heart. Why does someone have to be better or worse, Why can't I just be me. Why am I treated like I dirtied your shirt. Like I'm unclean. I am not your stain! Why do I have to die, I just want to live! Maybe it's you who's actually fading away...... Don't project that on me. Clean up your own mess.

LIGHTENING STRIKES

I've been waiting for you can't you hear me thundering

You are the most complete person I've ever encountered in my life!

Can't you see the storm coming:

Call me crazy but if I had to give up EVERYTHING to see you smile and wake up to your heart it's totally worth embracing no matter the storm.

It's raining now:

You are as rare as they come, you are worth, noting even documenting for a lifetime. Can't you feel the emotion pouring down its heavy and intense.

Look at the Lightning:

*Did you happen to notice our spark, I see it in your eyes you thought you could hide it, but now the flash of lightening reflects what you can't hide anymore, the secret to your heart!!! Do you go in the house for cover, or stay outside and embrace the spectacle that is awaiting you. That is for you to choose, the storm if you let it will pass because this type of lightning only **strikes** once!*

LEGENDS OF THE
FALL (SEASON)

I use to be a fan of all the hotness until I figured out it was just superficial. You don't always get to spring into action if it's too snowy or rainy to do anything. Don't ask me if I want summer of it because by then it's dried up and nothing is green anymore and....uh.... it's too crowded so now it's hotter or is that just me getting pissed off. I guess I loved it when I was younger that was the case, but now it just makes my blood boil because every cost (gas, flights, heat) is too high.... Fast forward to December, when I winter the house it is still too cold to want to do anything but sleep and bundle up. You can only be outside so much before you need to warm up and driving or should I say sliding on it isn't any better. Who wants to play slip and slide all winter. I didn't think so, that can't be the best seasoning out there. I only need to see one snow flake please don't sprinkle me with anymore. So let's fall back in line here. You don't have to take my word for it but I Autumn-matically know you will understand. When you wake up and the temperatures are cool or a little brisk but warm up enough for you to take the morning stroll or an afternoon picnic or hike and if it's not just the air relaxing on your face, the sun is being kind today and loving with gentle warmness. You get to see the kids and animals play little more with still calmness. Last, the trees in some places decide to forever sunset by dressing up in yellow, green, brown red and orange to get your attention. Orange you glad it's not hot anymore. You can't help but FALL for it!

NO MORE WORDS

I've said all that I can say. As illustrious as I would want to construct things, I decided against dragging out the ridiculous extension of eloquently worded nonsense. That relatively speaking is irrelevant and pretentious yet descriptive in nature. How captivating does that sound to acutely rationalize, what so deeply intrenched in a momentous approval from others, that I forget the message. Why do I need to use all those words for something so simple. I should just slow it down and make it easier to understand. Never stopping to think. I could just summarize this all in a few words. So let's try this. I hope you enjoyed. I hope something resonated with you. I did this for myself. I hope you can see the light in yourself. Doesn't matter what others think. Just do you, find your gem in your eye. Pursue it no matter what. Believe in you, Be you... do you... for you... love yourself... go do it... just try... right now.... Use.... Your..... Gem... **No.... More   Words.......**

Just Actions

RHYTHM

Zoom Zoom Zoom
Boom Boom Boom
Bop Bop Bop
Pop Pop Pop
Hot Hot Hot
drop drop drop
Smooth........ smooth…….smooth……..
Groove. ……Groove….. Groove………
Boom Pop. Boom Pop
Zoom Bop. Zoom Bop
Zoom bop hot boom pop drop
Pop smooth ……..Suave….. Pop Groove…… Suave
Hot ….Groove…. Suave…… Hot Smooth….. Suave
Drop…. Drop Drop Drop Drop
Drop…. Drop Drop Drop Drop
Snap Snap Snap
TAP TAP TAP
Paddy wack… Paddy wack
yeaha-heah… yeaha-heah
Run it back now y'all

ABOUT THE AUTHOR

Rollo Reese

Rollo Reese is a creative writer, world traveler and former financial services manager. Rollo was born in Omaha Nebraska, but has grown up in Colorado, Nebraska, and Georgia. He currently resides in Arizona. He has worked in the financial services industry for 20 years, starting at the age of 19. In his spare time, he loves expressing himself in creative avenues that include video and writting). When he's not creative writing, he loves to travel and has gone to over 35 countries and counting. Rollo also runs a podcast and has a youtube channel dedicated to travel.

You can chat with Rollo Reese on instagram @colorollo, on Linkedin @http://linkedin.com/in/rollo-reese-1b692951

The **Gem** in eye
Created by a **Gemini**
Playing brain games (the **gym** in I)
Hope this book inspires the **gem** in you!!! "

www.ingramcontent.com/pod-product-compliance
Lightning Source LLC
Chambersburg PA
CBHW051431090426
42737CB00014B/2919